Sassy Lassy

7 Year Old Edition

TRY NOT TO LAUGH CHALLENGE ™

Try Not To Laugh Challenge
BONUS PLAY

Join our Joke Club and get the Bonus Play PDF!

Simply send us an email to:

TNTLPublishing@gmail.com

and you will get the following:

• 10 Hilarious BONUS Jokes

• An entry in our Monthly Giveaway of a $50 Amazon Gift card!

We draw a new winner each month and will contact you via email!

 Good luck!

Welcome to the
Try Not To Laugh Challenge
✧ Sassy Lassy Edition! ✧

RULES OF THE GAME:

★ Grab a friend or family member, a pen/pencil, and your comedic skills! Determine who will be "Lassy 1" and "Lassy 2".

★ Take turns reading the jokes aloud to each other, and check the box next to each joke you get a laugh from! Each laugh box is worth 1 point, and the pages are labeled to instruct and guide when it is each player's turn.

★ Once you have both completed telling jokes in the round, tally up your laugh points and mark it down on each score page! There is a total of 10 Rounds.

★ Play as many rounds as you like! Once you reach the last round, Round 10, tally up ALL points from the previous rounds to determine who is the CHAMPION LAUGH MASTER!

★ Round 11 - The Tie-Breaker Round.

In the event of a tie, proceed to Round 11. This round will be 'Winner Takes All!', so whoever scores more laugh points in this round alone, is crowned the CHAMPION LAUGH MASTER!

TIP: Use an expressive voice, facial expressions, and even silly body movement to really get the most out of each joke and keep the crowd laughing!

Now, it's time to play!

ROUND

Lassy 1

What is Elsa's favorite part of baking cupcakes?
Frosting them, of course!

LAUGH

Why did the fairy have trouble paying attention?
Her head was always in the clouds.

LAUGH

Where does a Yeti keep its money?
In a snowbank!

LAUGH

Why do mermaids work together in their garden?
Everyone could use a little KELP!

LAUGH

Lassy 1

How many unicorns did it take to screw in a lightbulb?

None! Unicorns don't have hands!

 LAUGH

What does a raincloud do when he's mad at you?

He storms out!

 LAUGH

Why don't mermaids need glue?

Because fish-sticks!

 LAUGH

What does a ghost get his girlfriend on Valentine's Day?

A BOO-quet.

  LAUGH

Pass the book to Lassy 2! ➞

11

Lassy 2

What is a cupcake's favorite season?
SPRING-kles!

LAUGH

Which candy aced the test?
The Smartee.

LAUGH

How do you make sure you don't slip on a banana?
Just keep your eyes PEELED.

LAUGH

What is a cow's favorite part of the carnival?
The Moooo-n bounce!

LAUGH

Lassy 2

What do you call an alien that carries its young in a pouch?

A MARS-supial.

☐ LAUGH

What do you need if it isn't clean enough?

MORE-maids.

☐ LAUGH

What does a butterfly sleep on?

A cater-PILLOW.

☐ LAUGH

What do you call it when you eat fried chicken in the pool?

Water wings!

☐ LAUGH

Time to add up your points! →

SCORE BOARD

Add up each Lassy's laugh points for this round!

Lassy 1

$\underline{\quad\quad} / 8$

Total

Lassy 2

$\underline{\quad\quad} / 8$

Total

ROUND WINNER

ROUND

Lassy 1

Why was Dracula nervous at his softball game?

It was his turn to go up to BAT!

LAUGH

What do you get when you step on a spider's home?

Webbed feet.

LAUGH

What do you call a cologne meant to calm stressed-out cats?

PURR-fume.

LAUGH

What kind of cracker shouldn't be eaten?

A firecracker!

LAUGH

Lassy 1

What kind of bean goes well with peanut butter?

JELLY bean.

LAUGH

Why did the chicken go out of town for a long weekend?

She was scared of FRY-day!

LAUGH

What do you call a bee with curly hair that spins around?

A FRIZ-bee!

LAUGH

What kind of cream doesn't go well with coffee?

Shaving cream.

LAUGH

Pass the book to Lassy 2! →

Lassy 2

What do you call a science fair project trying to create new flavors of gum?

Ex-SPEARMINT.

 LAUGH

Why do pigs always throw their dirty clothes on the floor?

They are scared of the HAM-per!

 LAUGH

What is the most flexible kind of dessert?

A banana SPLIT.

 LAUGH

What's a bug's favorite thing to drink?

Beetle Juice!

 LAUGH

Lassy 2

What kind of waterfowl is always a hit at parties?
A ba-LOON!

☐ LAUGH

What do you call a plant's home?
A Greenhouse.

☐ LAUGH

Why does a fairy have to clean her house often?
Fairy dust, duh.

☐ LAUGH

What piece of furniture is always starting drama with the others?
The WAR-drobe.

☐ LAUGH

Time to add up your points! ➔

SCORE BOARD

Add up each Lassy's laugh points
for this round!

Lassy 1

/8
_____
Total

Lassy 2

/8
_____
Total

_____

ROUND WINNER

ROUND

3

Lassy 1

How do you get chickens for buy-one-get-one?
You need a COOP-on!

☐ LAUGH

What kind of tar do people enjoy?
A gui-TAR.

☐ LAUGH

What's the sweetest kind of factory?
The Cheesecake Factory!

☐ LAUGH

Why did the queen have her horseman wear a glow-in-the-dark helmet?
She wanted a KNIGHT light!

☐ LAUGH

Lassy 1

What kind of vegetable gives the best haircut?

A par-SNIP.

LAUGH

How does the ocean say goodbye?

"SEA you later!"

LAUGH

Why did the piece of wood leave the party?

He was board.

LAUGH

What kind of park has no swings?

A water park!

LAUGH

Pass the book to Lassy 2! ➜

23

Lassy 2

What is a tornado's favorite party game?
Twister!

LAUGH

Why did the drummer have long hair?
Because he really liked BANGS!

LAUGH

What do you call it when a trampoline snaps?
Spring break.

LAUGH

What do you call it when a computer has a large lunch?
A mega-bite!

LAUGH

Lassy 2

Why was the sun so famous?
Well, it is a super-STAR!

LAUGH

What did the mermaid say to her friend after a fight?
"We're FIN-ished!"

LAUGH

Which flowers give the best kisses?
Two-lips.

LAUGH

What did the unicorn say to the fairy when she asked for a ride?
"Neigh."

LAUGH

Time to add up your points! →

SCORE BOARD

Add up each Lassy's laugh points
for this round!

Lassy 1 /8
Total

Lassy 2 /8
Total

ROUND WINNER

ROUND 4

Lassy 1

Why did the mermaid read the newspaper?

She wanted to keep up with the CURRENT events.

LAUGH

What do you call a frog's poop?

A toadstool.

LAUGH

Why didn't the moon want dessert?

It was already FULL!

LAUGH

Which dog lives underground?

A Prairie dog!

LAUGH

Lassy 1

What is an elf's favorite type of car?
TOY-ota.

LAUGH

Which animal is the hardest to hide alongside in the bushes?
A hedge-HOG!

LAUGH

How has the TV been doing since we lost the remote?
It's been feeling out of control.

☐
LAUGH

What do you call an old unicorn?
A rhino!

LAUGH

Pass the book to Lassy 2! →

Lassy 2

Why don't mermaids eat peanut butter and jelly sandwiches?

Because the jelly would sting!

LAUGH

What's a dog's favorite kind of cheese?

MUTT-zorella.

LAUGH

Who do fish see when they are hurt?

The Nurse shark.

LAUGH

What kind of drum cannot be played?

An eardrum!

LAUGH

Lassy 2

What do evil villains read to their children at bedtime?
Nursery CRIMES.

LAUGH

Why do aliens need vacuum cleaners?
To clean up all the stardust!

LAUGH

Why did the teacher get a slushie machine for the first day of school?
She wanted help break the ice!

☐
LAUGH

Which fruit do fish like most?
WATER-melon.

☐
LAUGH

Time to add up your points! →

31

SCORE BOARD

Add up each Lassy's laugh points for this round!

Lassy 1

/8
Total

Lassy 2

/8
Total

ROUND WINNER

ROUND 5

Lassy 1

Why do teddy bears love buffets?

It's the best place to get stuffed!

LAUGH

What kind of insect breathes fire when he's angry?

A Dragon-fly!

LAUGH

How can you tell how old a letter is?

Check it's post-AGE!

LAUGH

What do you call a sleepover for trees?

A LUMBER party!

LAUG

Lassy 1

What is a park ranger's favorite dessert?
Chocolate mousse. (Moose)

LAUGH

Where did the horse go to work on his balance?
The stable.

LAUGH

Where do ghosts train to haunt people?
Booo-t camp!

☐
LAUGH

What did the blanket say when the bed asked for help?
"I got it covered!"

☐
LAUGH

Pass the book to Lassy 2! →

35

Lassy 2

Why does Flounder always come watch Ariel sing?

He is her #1 FIN!

LAUGH

How is the tooth fairy similar to a lie detector?

She always uncovers the TOOTH!

LAUGH

What do clouds wear in their hair?

Rain-BOWS.

LAUGH

What kind of magical creature helps give the meaning of words?

A Diction-Fairy!

LAUGH

Lassy 2

What do you call an asteroid made of beef?
MEAT-eor!

☐ LAUGH

Why are cacti good at sewing?
They have lots of needles!

☐ LAUGH

What's a tree's favorite game to play?
Wood You Rather?

☐ LAUGH

How does a rose ride a unicycle?
She petals!

☐ LAUGH

Time to add up your points! →

37

SCORE BOARD

Add up each Lassy's laugh points
for this round!

Lassy 1

/8

Total

Lassy 2

/8

Total

ROUND WINNER

ROUND

6

Lassy 1

What do indifferent vegetables say?
"I do not CARROT-all."

LAUGH

Which lamp is considered the hottest?
A LAVA lamp!

LAUGH

What do you get when you cross a cow with a cyclops?
Bulls-eye!

LAUGH

Why are kangaroo's great at grocery shopping?
They never forget their pouches!

LAUGH

40

Lassy 1

Which type of chair loves music?

The Rockin' chair.

LAUGH

What did the chef say when asked about dessert?

"It's a piece of cake."

LAUGH

Did you hear about the kid who fell asleep on a coral reef tour?

She was SNORE-keling!

LAUGH

What do you call someone with fast food on the side of their face?

Cheeseburg-EARS!

LAUGH

Pass the book to Lassy 2! →

Lassy 2

What do tools eat with their Chinese food?
Soy Saws.

LAUGH

What's the loneliest kind of land?
I-sland.

LAUGH

What did the lettuce say to his friends in a time of chaos?
"ROMAINE calm!"

LAUGH

When you come out with a breakfast cookbook, how do you thank your mom for all her help?
In the EGG-knowledgements!

LAUGH

Lassy 2

What is the cutest kind of sleep?

A cat nap!

 LAUGH

Which type of tube offers hours of entertainment?

You-TUBE. ♥

 LAUGH

What game do you play when someone is at your door?

Guess Who!

 LAUGH

What band doesn't play music?

A headband.

 LAUGH

Time to add up your points! →

SCORE BOARD

Add up each Lassy's laugh points for this round!

Lassy 1   /8
                 Total

Lassy 2   /8
                 Total

ROUND WINNER

44

ROUND 7

Lassy 1

What makes you cry but isn't mean or sad?
An onion!

LAUGH

What has multiple lives but isn't in a video game?
A cat!

LAUGH

Which insect always remembers to take their vitamins in the morning?
A PILL-bug.

LAUGH

What do you call it when a tiny bird plays percussion in your band?
Humdrum!

LAUG

Lassy 1

What kind of hawk doesn't fly?
A Mo-hawk!

LAUGH

What does a lamb always bring to a slumber party?
Her SHEEP-ing bag!

LAUGH

Which lid is impossible to lose?
Your eye-LID.

☐
LAUGH

What do rainbows write with?
Colored pencils!

LAUGH

Pass the book to Lassy 2! →

Lassy 2

How did the baker get so rich?
He made DOUGH all day!

LAUGH

Why is cheddar so good at math?
He's a Cheese Whiz.

LAUGH

How do vegetables send texts?
By using their CELERY phones.

LAUGH

What do you call it when you combine money and lemons together?
Sour-dough.

LAUG

Lassy 2

What is a rabbit's favorite instrument?
A HARE-monica.

LAUGH

What kind of bills do people love getting?
Dollar bills!

LAUGH

Which doctor is actually bad for you?
Dr. Pepper

LAUGH

What is a fluffy, crying hamster's favorite sport?
Soft BAWL.

LAUGH

Time to add up your points! →

SCORE BOARD

Add up each Lassy's laugh points for this round!

Lassy 1

/8

Total

Lassy 2

/8

Total

ROUND WINNER

ROUND

Lassy 1

What's the Jedi's favorite weapon in the office?
The screen-saber!

LAUGH

What should you do to the towel if you like it?
Put a WRING on it!

LAUGH

Yoga claims it is good for downward facing dogs, but that's a STRETCH!

LAUGH

Why was the doorbell upset at the mailman?
He knocked it before he tried it!

LAUGH

Lassy 1

What is Elsa's favorite food to eat for dinner?

Brrrr-gers!

LAUGH

What do you call a unicorn in a zoo?

The mane attraction!

LAUGH

What is the saddest dessert?

TEAR-amisu.

LAUGH

What do you call someone who searches the ocean floor for ice cream cones?

A SCOOP-a diver!

LAUGH

Pass the book to Lassy 2! →

Lassy 2

What did the fully bloomed flower say to the baby flower?

"What's up, bud?"

LAUGH

Why did the boy go to outer space for his health?

He was tired of being UNDER the weather!

LAUGH

What type of instrument does a unicorn like to play?

The horn!

LAUGH

The soccer players went to a birthday party yesterday. They had a BALL!

LAUGH

Lassy 2

What's a square's favorite board game?
Connect Four.

LAUGH

Why wasn't the farmer worried that the crops were late?
She knew they would TURNIP sooner or later!

LAUGH

What is a fairy's favorite drawing tool?
The Magic Marker.

LAUGH

Who is the unicorn's dentist?
The Tooth Fairy!

LAUGH

Time to add up your points! →

SCORE BOARD

Add up each Lassy's laugh points
for this round!

Lassy 1

/8
___
Total

Lassy 2

/8
___
Total

ROUND WINNER

ROUND 9

Lassy 1

What do you call it when a snail travels into the past?

SLIME Travel.

LAUGH

How do you cut a wave in half?

With a SEA-saw!

LAUGH

What do you call a sandwich at school?

A SUB-stitute teacher!

LAUGH

How do cats gossip?

They whisker!

LAUG

Lassy 1

What do you call someone who falls asleep in a suit?

A Dapper Napper.

LAUGH

Why was the valley laughing so hard at the hill?

He thought it looked HILL-arious!

LAUGH

What board game has grumpy hippopotamuses?

Hangry Hangry Hippos!

LAUGH

What did the social pony always say?

"Hay!"

LAUGH

Pass the book to Lassy 2! →

Lassy 2

Why do buckets hate being left in the sun?
Because they're usually PAIL.

LAUGH

What do mermaids use as currency?
Sand dollars.

LAUGH

Why did three subtract two?
He wanted to be number one!

LAUGH

What was the boy seen chasing after?
His running shoes!

LAUG

Lassy 2

What does an Australian use to open a door?
A Cri-KEY.

 LAUGH

How does a witch get you to fall in love with her?
She sweeps you off your feet!

 LAUGH

Why is Belle so strict?
She does everything by the book!

 LAUGH

What's a unicorn's favorite dance?
The poke-a.

 LAUGH

Time to add up your points! →

61

SCORE BOARD

Add up each Lassy's laugh points
for this round!

Lassy 1

/8

Total

Lassy 2

/8

Total

ROUND WINNER

ROUND

10

Lassy 1

What do you call a horse in prison?
A zebra.

LAUGH

Why did the motorcycle have to take a rest?
It was two TIRE-d.

LAUGH

Which part of the computer opens doors?
The KEY-board!

LAUGH

What do wood boards do for fun?
They make PLANK calls!

LAUGH

Lassy 1

Why did the kid pour milk on the street?

She wanted to see the Milky Way.

LAUGH

What kind of table do most kids not like?

A vege-TABLE.

LAUGH

Why was the earthquake always laughing?

He liked to crack up!

LAUGH

What do you call it when a shoe is busy?

Tied up!

LAUGH

Pass the book to Lassy 2! →

Lassy 2

Why did Barbie always show up late for dinner?

Because she always got DOLL-ed up!

O LAUGH

How do you celebrate the 20th letter?

With a 'T' party!

O LAUGH

What's a rainbow's favorite reading material?

Coloring books.

O LAUGH

How do you weigh a mermaid?

On a scale!

O LAUG

Lassy 2

Why shouldn't you be a drummer in the same band as your crush?

Your heart will keep skipping a beat!

LAUGH

Why are some trees really funny?

They're NUTS!

LAUGH

How did the tooth fairy fix her broken wand?

Toothpaste.

LAUGH

What is under ur mouth?

Ur-chin!

LAUGH

Time to add up your points! →

SCORE BOARD

Add up each Lassy's laugh points
for this round!

Lassy 1   /8
            Total

Lassy 2   /8
            Total

ROUND WINNER

Add up all your points from each round.
The Lassy with the most points is crowned

The Laugh Master!

In the event of a tie, continue to
Round 11 – The Tie-Breaker Round!

Lassy 1

_____

Grand Total

Lassy 2

_____

Grand Total

THE LAUGH MASTER

ROUND

11

Tie-Breaker
(Winner Take All!)

Lassy 1

What does a kitten write in her diary?
PAW-etry.

LAUGH

How did the unicorn get around traffic?
It used its horn!

LAUGH

How do you get the postal service to let you send yourself through the mail?
STAMP your feet!

LAUG

What does a bobblehead do when she needs to unwind?
She takes a BOBBLE bath.

LAUG

Lassy 1

What kind of vegetable always gets dizzy?
SPIN-ach!

LAUGH

Where do fish superheroes live?
Cape Cod.

LAUGH

What do you call a famous hog's autograph?
A PIG-nature.

LAUGH

Why didn't the bear trust the trout?
He thought it seemed a little fishy...

LAUGH

Pass the book to Lassy 2!

Lassy 2

Why did Cinderella throw the pumpkin?

The prince told her to have a smashing time!

LAUGH

What planet has the best lullabies?

NAP-tune.

LAUGH

Why didn't the farmer like his new cow?

He missed the UDDER one!

LAUG

What kind of bean can you never trust?

A LIE-ma bean!

LAUG

Lassy 2

What body part would complete a fairy's story?

A tale.

☐ LAUGH

What did the unicorn say to her boyfriend?

"You're my mane man."

☐ LAUGH

Where does a cat keep all her favorite things to scratch?

In her CLAW-set!

☐ LAUGH

What is a pink bird's preferred position in soccer?

Flamin-GOALIE!

☐ LAUGH

Time to add up your points! ➜

Add up all your points from the Tie-Breaker Round.
The Lassy with the most points is crowned
The Laugh Master!

Lassy 1

/8
Total

Lassy 2

/8
Total

_____

THE LAUGH MASTER

Check out our

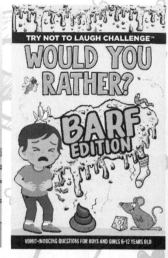

Visit our Amazon Store at

other joke books!

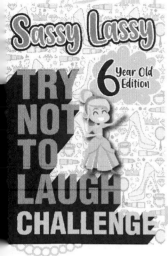

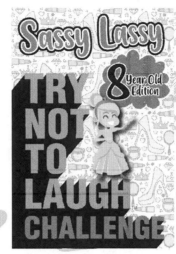

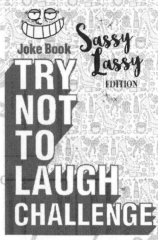

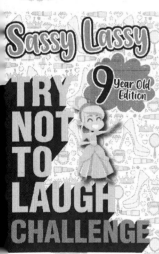

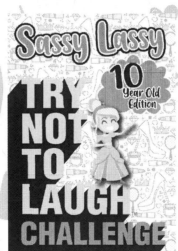

www.Amazon.com/author/CrazyCorey